ANCH(

BY TRUST

STORIES OF FAITH IN A GOD WORTH TRUSTING

SOLA MACAULAY

Unless otherwise noted, all Scripture is taken from the King James Version of the Bible.

Paperback: ISBN 978-1725588363

Jedidiah Publications Limited

jedidiahpubltd@gmail.com
+234-7080317274

Cover design by Ibraheem Akeem

Book Layout ©2017 BookDesignTemplates.com

Anchored By Trust/ Sola Macaulay. —1st edition.

Dedicated to every woman holding on to God,
fully anchored by trust.

Never be afraid to trust an unknown future to a known God.

—CORRIE TEN BOON

Contents

Preface

Dear Reader,

Walking with God requires absolute trust. Trust in Him, His words, His promises, His goodness, and His name. When we truly understand the character of God, we can rest in Him. That rest in God dispels doubts.

Thou wilt keep him in perfect peace, whose mind is stayed on thee: because he trusteth in thee.
— *Isaiah 59:1(King James Version, KJV)*

Often, we struggle with the issue of trust because people have failed us and there are trying times capable of eroding trust and confidence in God. We are only human. However, in our walk with God, we err when we relate with God like we do people.

God is never too busy to hear us when we call. His methods may be unorthodox, but His response and timing are impeccable. God understands us and knows what we need and how to best reach us.

Sometimes we attempt to trust God but with a Plan B, in case God doesn't answer us the way we expect The truth is that we cannot walk with

God successfully without settling the trust issue. The scriptures tell us:

But without faith it is impossible to please him: for he that cometh to God must believe that God is, and that He is a rewarder of them that diligently seek Him. Hebrews 11:6 (KJV)

If we want to see God's hand in our lives we have to trust Him completely. God cannot do anything without faith or trust. Our lack of trust restricts God from unleashing His faithfulness and goodness in our lives. God loves us unequivocally. He ever keeps His promises. We just need to let go and trust Him.

Trusting God will mean learning to wait for His divine timing. It is in that season of waiting that our faith may falter because circumstances around us dictate hopelessness. Yet, it is at this crucial time that we need to grab hold of Him.

In writing this book I have asked myself these questions: Have I always trusted God totally? The answer is No. Have I been tempted to give up on God? Yes, many times. Have I learned to trust God ultimately? Yes.
Has God come through for me? Oh yes.
I'm I still on the trust journey? Yes.

Is God truly trustworthy? Yes and an absolute Yes.

You see, no matter how bad things look, your safest anchor is in God. He is the only one capable of holding the thread of your life together when things are crumbling around.

You are not alone in your trust journey. As we share our stories of trust and how we learned to trust God in our unique situations, I hope that even before you get to the end of this book, your trust in God would have been reawakened and strengthened.

He is God and He is more than able to perform and exceed our expectations:

Now unto him that is able to do exceeding abundantly above all that we ask or think, according to the power that worketh in us. Ephesians 3:20

Trusting God does not mean throwing out our reasoning capacity, but submitting it to God. Trusting God requires patience. God's timing is God's timing. God's method is God's method. We need to accept both His timing and His method. Trusting God correctly brings complete rest. He has never failed us.

There remaineth therefore a rest to the people of God.
For he that is entered into his rest, he also hath ceased
from his own works, as God did from his. Hebrew 4:9-10

So please:

Trust in the Lord with all thine heart; and lean not unto
thine own understanding. Proverbs 3:5 (KJV)

Let us walk you through our trust process. Our hope, our strength, our life and our trust is anchored in Him.

Many blessings,
Sola Macaulay
   June 2018

Acknowledgement

When I contacted these wonderful women to join me in sharing our stories of 'trust in God', they, with much enthusiasm jumped on board. My heartfelt thanks goes to my sisters/friends who chose to share their trust stories in this book. I appreciate everyone one of you and thank you for going on this journey with me. Love you loads.

In putting the book together and giving it a smooth flowing prose, through a collaborative effort, my thanks goes to Nkoyo Itegboje who did the first phase of editing and my editor Joy Ehonwa who put the finishing touch to this book.

I am grateful to God Almighty for giving us a platform to write and share of our walk with Him.

CHAPTER 1

An Anchor For My Future

rowing up, I saw faith and hope in God modelled for me in the best way possible. As the last child of a single mother, I had no real knowledge of our challenges or how tight things were. All I knew was that my mum prayed and prayed and prayed. I figured it was just the way things were supposed to be. Nothing ever seemed too difficult or impossible to navigate. If there ever was a problem, her first words were that God would work it out.

She taught us to read and memorize scripture. She would come into our room at all hours of the night, praying for my siblings and me, touching our foreheads one after another. She worked tirelessly at church, praying for others, serving on one committee or the other. I don't think she was necessarily trying to drum something into us; she wasn't trying to make us turn out a certain way, she was just living the life she knew to live, diligently and unpretentiously.

And that was why it all stuck. As I grew older, the words, 'Lord, help me' were always on my lips no matter the challenge I encountered, from figuring out how to do a math problem on an exam (I hate math!) to getting ready to speak to a crowd (I've always been on the shy side).

I learned how to navigate life by simply reaching out to my Father in heaven. It was a special relationship. I didn't have a dad, so it was easy to give God that space in my heart.

I also learned to give thanks to God no matter how small the victory or how mundane the accomplishment. I learned that from my mother. We were always praying and giving thanks. She would pray and thank God as soon as she stepped foot in the house after a long day. She would pray when we got into the car about to embark on a trip. I guess it just came naturally for her.

Needless to say, my journey of learning to trust God started with my mum. The truth, however, is that everyone runs her own race. My mum's influence was incredible, but I didn't realize until later (as an adult) that God was working things out so I could learn to trust Him for myself.

You see my childhood was kind of peculiar. I don't remember us having outings or activities like most kids had. My siblings went off to boarding school at some point and, as the last child; I was left with Mum. I stayed home a lot because my mom worked long hours. I was often in the company of the neighbours and the occasional uncle and aunt. There wasn't much going on around me, and as a result there started to be a lot going on inside me. I read voraciously and daydreamed like my life depended on it. I also read my Bible a lot and pondered God and His vastness.

It wasn't until I became an adult that I got the sense that as a child, those early years were lonely and hard but not worthless. I believe God literally impressed Himself upon my little heart. I knew I had to walk the path of faith. There was never a question as to God's grace, love or faithfulness. It was a given.

Adult problems

We all know how life creeps up on you. You think you have things figured out. You get your degree, begin to map out a strategy for your life or at least a progression that makes sense to you, but then things take an unfamiliar turn and you wonder which part of your story was torn out of the pages of life.

My issues with fully trusting God started as I pondered my future. I'm not exactly a big picture thinker, I prefer to work out details and see how things come together. However the reverse is the case when it comes to my future; I prefer to have an idea of my next four or five steps. I was standing on promises that the Lord had spoken into my life and was very expectant to see them manifest. But alas, the waiting never seemed to end! I manufactured deadlines in my mind of when God would show up and make things happen for me. I wanted an extraordinary experience as I got ready to go to university to become a doctor but I barely made it into the Microbiology department. I grieved over that seeming failure for months but soon began to accept the way things were. What I didn't realize was that the seeds of doubt as to whether God's word would prove true had been planted in my heart. I still loved my Father, and I knew He loved me. But could I always count on His promises to come to pass? I hesitated on that one.

I graduated from school and entered the workforce with so much fear for my future. There I was, a microbiologist by training, yet I had no desire to work in a laboratory or even pursue anything in the field. But what was I to do?
Every prayer for direction felt like it hit the roof and fell back on my head. I had never been more confused in my life. I wanted answers. I wanted to know what my future would look like.
Despite my declaration that I trusted God and believed Him wholeheartedly, I had forgotten the very thing He had told me about this issue in the past.

A word at every point in time

I was probably in my third year at the university when this happened. I had learned about purpose and passion and that, to succeed, you had to have a solid vision of what you were working towards. I looked inward and sincerely, I couldn't latch on to anything. I had wanted to be a doctor, but that dream tanked. I was studying microbiology but saw no future in it. At the time I had discovered my love for writing but I was too inexperienced to see it as any kind of advantage. So, what was my purpose? Why was I here? What was I to do with my life?

I decided to take a few days to pray and ask God these pertinent questions to which I needed answers or else I would lose my mind. Now that I think about it, I expected God to have simply laughed at or ignored my silliness. But He did something awesome. He sent me a word!

I was leaving the chapel one fine evening after a service when a friend walked up to me. She had been at our sister campus visiting some of our mutual friends, and one of them had asked her to relay a message to me from, guess who? Our Father in heaven Himself. The message was simple: Do not worry about purpose. Just do whatever I ask you to do at every point in time.

You have no idea how elated I was at that moment! God had heard my prayers in my little room and sent an answer through someone I hadn't spoken to in years. Someone who had no idea what I had been asking or praying about! If I ever had any doubt that He loved me unconditionally, that moment washed away all of that foolishness. I floated around in that euphoria for as long as I could but unfortunately, I'm human. Life happens and you begin to wonder if God sees you or even has a plan for you.

Years later, as a graduate, I found myself praying concerning the very thing He had assured me about years earlier. I was still unsure in many ways; nevertheless, I started to take steps to move my life forward. I gathered my trust for God from all the places it had been scattered as fear assailed my heart and left my spirit heavy and battle-weary.

For the next few years, I worked at different jobs, picking up expertise in things that would somehow define my future. I did the things I knew to do: show up, be diligent and do the work.

This is not to say that I didn't feel my trust waning at certain times. I did. The more uncertain things became, the more I struggled to hold on to His word for me. I learned how to go to battle to defend my faith in God. It was a continuous journey.

A dream, unburied

Many years later, long after I had buried my dream of getting a Master's degree abroad, life handed me an opportunity to go down that path. I say I had buried that dream because prior to this time I had received admission to a school in the UK and a prestigious one in Nigeria but never could attend because I had no money. I applied for scholarship after scholarship but nothing ever worked out. So, when presented with the opportunity to apply to a school in the US, my answer was no. You see, even though I still had the desire to travel abroad and see the world, I had given up on the dream after being disappointed twice. Yet, this thought kept coming to me.

So, I started to pray. 'Lord, do you want me to do this? Should I apply to this school? Where will I find the money? What if this is another fruitless pursuit?'

I did apply because I felt God nudging me in that direction. I had a few months to get my application in, be accepted (or not), get the necessary supporting papers, put together money for tuition (at least the first semester) and obtain a visa.

It all happened. Months later, I stood at Murtala Mohammed Airport waving goodbye to my family and boarding a plane for the second time in my life. (There's a story about the first one. Hilarious stuff!)

All these happened while I harboured a nagging fear in my mind. What if I had no money to pay for the second semester, or the third, or the fourth? What would happen then? Was I foolish to take this journey without all the millions of naira I needed in my bank account? Was I going to return home having been expelled for not paying tuition? What would I do then? How would I start to pick up the pieces of my life? I had almost forgotten my Father's nudge that this was His idea; that He had my back and things would work out for good.

I landed in Texas, went straight to grad school and experienced the biggest culture shock ever! Not only was I in a different part of the world where people didn't understand my kind of English, I was studying a course I had no background or prior knowledge in (except for a few years of work experience). However, I was determined to succeed. I studied hard, locked myself in my closet in the winter to keep warm (as my roommate and I couldn't afford to use the heater and rack up high electricity bills) and gave it my all. Yet, a voice in my head never stopped taunting me. 'Where will you find the money? Do you know many people like you have had to go back home because they couldn't pay up?'

I was afraid, to say the least. I gave in to fear and found my trust waning once again. I tried to get a job on campus but got rejected at every turn. Not that a campus job—the only kind I could get at the time because of my student status—could pay enough to cover my tuition, but anything was welcome. I slowly burned through my savings as one month rolled into the next.

During my second semester, I got invited to a school 'ring' ceremony but couldn't attend as I had no money for the ring. I kept looking for scholarships, trusting that that way I could get the funds to pay for my remaining semesters, but the rejections kept coming. I wanted a big miracle, something that would blow the socks off everyone who heard…yet nothing happened.

I would sign into the student portal just to look at the amount of money I owed, and my heart would sink every time. Then one day, I signed in and was shocked at what I saw. My tuition had been reduced by half. I owed less than the full amount! How did that happen? I learned later that one of the third-party school scholarships I had applied for had awarded me $1000 and it also came with a 50% tuition reduction. No kidding! I rolled on the floor of our little apartment. My Mum who was with me at the time did the same. We sang, we laughed and most importantly we prayed and praised God!

A few weeks later, before the second semester began, my fiancé and I got married. Thanks to our owambe 'spraying' custom and gifts from friends and family, we were able to get a significant amount of money. He had also gotten a job, so we were earning some money. We put all that together and were able to cover the remainder of the tuition for that semester.

My second year came around, and somehow my family was able to raise the money for tuition. I was praying for a miracle, and God handed it to me in the form of my amazing family who stood beside me through this wild ride. I still had one more semester to go. We kept burning through our savings and had no money for anything else.

I soon started to look for an internship opportunity as I was now legally allowed to work outside of the campus. I applied to dozens of companies but kept getting rejected. This time, I checked myself every time I started to complain about my situation or doubt that God could come through for me. I was in my third semester after all and hadn't been kicked out yet.

I applied for a copywriter job in a big cosmetics company, kept my fingers crossed, and prayed that this one would work. One day my phone rang and a lady from the company asked to set up a phone interview. I was so excited I nearly fell off my bed.

I studied and practiced for the interview. Then she called sometime before the interview day to say she was sorry, the people in the department had some meeting or the other and couldn't take the interview but would I come in to interview for another position? I wasn't sure whether to be excited or disappointed. I went for the interview and met this kind woman who asked me questions about my skills, my background and experience, looked over my portfolio and promptly gave me her number and asked me to call if I ever needed anything.

I was grateful for her kindness but I wasn't sure what to make of it. Did I get the job? Was she trying to let me down easy? I couldn't sleep that night, and many nights after that. I threw myself into work, writing papers and doing the required reading for my classes.

Then one day, while I was in the library, my phone rang. I ran out into the hallway to take the call and got the best news I had heard in a while. I got the job!

Long story short, it was a writing job that paid so well, I was able to pay the rest of my tuition and graduated with zero balance!

My Father came through. In His own way and at His own time and boy, was it perfect timing! I trust Him not because He paid my tuition and blessed me with a dream I had nurtured for years, but because He is who He is. He never fails. I don't know what the future holds and I'm fine with that (most times!) And, when I falter, I know His arms are big enough to catch me and place me back on solid ground. And for that, I am truly thankful!

Your turn

The truth is that we all have ideas about what we want our future to look like. If we didn't, we wouldn't be using our God-given imagination and ability to dream and create. The problem comes when we prioritize our 'dreams' over God's plans and promises for us; when we cling to our idea of the future so tightly that we refuse to hear His voice today; when we think His timing is slow, His processes tedious and not to our advantage.

Psalm 55:22 (New International Version, NIV) says, 'Cast your cares on the LORD and he will sustain you.'

Our God knows that you will have cares. You will have desires, wants, and things you want to achieve. He gave you that ability to dream, create and decide.

Remember what He told Abraham?

'As far as your eyes can see…'

Recognize that beneath your fears and worries about your future is simply a desire to see as far as you can. There's nothing wrong with that. However, remember what God said to Abraham.

 I am giving all this land, as far as you can see, to you and your descendants…

 Genesis 13:15(New Living Translation, NLT)

You will see, you must see, but only God can give it to you and make it happen (whatever 'it' means for you).

My prayer is that you will dream big and wide and bold, but more importantly, I pray you will look to Him who holds everything in His hands and trust Him to make your life work. The journey may be long, the process may be hard, but trust Him through it all. He knows what He's doing.

About this writer

REMI ROY is a writer and digital communications consultant passionate about spreading hope and the message of purpose through the written word.

Her experience as one who is saved by grace and empowered by God's love motivates her to share her story with the world.

She is the author of Ms. Unlikely and From the Sidelines, the editor of the Purpose Anthologies: A Collection of Personal Life Journeys and creator of the Follow Your Feet podcast.

You can connect with her at remiroyonline.com

Facebook: remiroyauthor

Instagram: @remiroy

CHAPTER 2

Why Carry This Pain If…

The pain was so real I could hardly sleep. I prayed and spoke in tongues intermittently for hours and truth be told, I felt a bit of relief whenever I prayed for about fifteen minutes and if I continued for say thirty to sixty minutes, the pain would almost disappear. Then I'd go back to sleep and another sharp pain would wake me up, then I'd pray in tongues, then I'd feel relief and this cycle continued till day break. I'm not sure I slept for one full hour between 11pm and 6am. By morning I sat up wondering why I felt worse even after seeing the doctor the day before. By now I'm sure you're wondering what was causing this pain. Let me start from the beginning.

I'd like to say that by the grace and mercy of God I've enjoyed divine health almost all my life. The only times I was in hospital for more than a few days was when I was about 15 or 16 where two non-malignant (non-cancerous) lumps had to be taken out of both breasts. The second time was when I had my first child; that pregnancy was particularly difficult and it ended up being a caesarean section. I've also had few (I can only remember three instances) cases of being rushed to the ER.

To the brief summary of my medical life, I should also add that I do not like hospital visits. For me, hospital visits should be reserved for outright emergencies. Note that this does not come from my Christian background in any way. Yes, my parents are Christians but they did not give their lives to Christ till my late teens. In fact my younger sister and I gave our lives to Christ (led to Him by my born again cousin living with us at the time) before I turned ten; my parents were okay with it but still didn't surrender their own lives to Christ until years later. I'm not sure how my dislike for hospital visits started; the only connection I can point to is that my parents leaned somewhat towards finding natural remedies within the house to treat minor ailments rather than rushing us to hospital for cold and catarrh symptoms. We rarely had malaria and when we did we only went to the hospital to get the right prescription.

This entire gist is so you can understand how upset I was to be having another sleepless night after a visit to the hospital, to treat my ear infection. Yes, the name behind the pain that caused me a sleepless night was an ear infection. It started about five days before my visit to the hospital. After having my shower, some water got lodged in my ear. I gently poked my forefinger in to try and open up my inner ear so the water could come out. One thing led to another and I found myself still tampering with my ear long after I'd gotten dressed. By the end of the day my ear throbbed with mild pain from all the poking.

Three days later the pain had become unbearable and had started affecting my sleep. It was on the fifth day my husband decided that we should go see a doctor. The waiting time to see the doctor felt like eternity mainly because of the splitting headache slashing through my head as we waited for my name to be called. The waiting time was no more than thirty minutes but I felt like I would pass out any moment. Even the steps I took were painful. Eventually, I got called and I explained everything to the doctor. He proceeded to examine my ear and his gentle touch sent daggers of pain to my brain, but I had to endure as he used his otoscope (an instrument designed for visual examination of the ear drum) to examine the insides of my ear. As he examined, he remained calm and his face even looked relaxed, but the words that came out of his mouth were not calming and definitely not relaxing. On the contrary his words got me quite disturbed. He said that it seemed like mixed debris of earwax, bits of torn flesh and blood had piled up, blocking my ear completely, so much so that he couldn't even see into my ear. He said it looked very bad and quite troubling. So he gave me some pain medication to help with the pain and an ear drop to help clear up the debris, with the hope that the ear could then be properly examined. I was to return to him in about three days.

So I went home and diligently took my medication as prescribed. Night time came and my sleep struggle resumed at an all time high; my fourth sleepless night in a row. The pain I felt before I saw the doctor seemed to have tripled. The ear drop prescribed also seemed to be aggravating the whole matter. Honestly to fully describe the torture and pain I was going through would be futile. This time I decided to add prayers alongside taking my medication. I was actually doing this before going to see the doctor, but it was difficult to pray while in pain so my prayer pattern during this period was not all that serious. However, having gone through four sleepless nights in a row, I determined in my heart that I would not have a fifth sleepless night. So when morning came I did a mental catalogue of what my options were and the only meaningful option that kept coming to my mind was to trust God for a solution. I know for a fact that faith comes by hearing and hearing the word of God. So I continued with my list of who I could listen to that would build my faith up to the required level for healing to occur.

One of my favourite pastimes is listening to randomly selected messages by various men of God, but when I'm at a crossroads in making a decision I often pick Pastor Keith Moore. His preaching style almost always touches me to my core and pushes me to becoming a doer of the word, not just a hearer. Plus his ministry's website offers free downloads on all his messages, some even dating back to the 1980s. I quickly went to his website to search out any sermons on healing; he had several but the one that jumped out at me was one titled "By His Stripes". In less than five minutes of listening, a newfound hope began to surge within me. There were so many key points raised, but I'll briefly mention the one that moved me to act.

His main scripture reference was Isaiah 53 and he attempted to break the whole chapter down, verse by verse. When he got to verses three and four, he pointed out that the words 'griefs' and 'sorrows' in those two verses are in other places of the King James Version (KJV), and is translated as sickness and pain respectively. So the real translation of Isaiah 53: 4 should be, "Surely He hath borne our sicknesses and carried our pains..." In other words, why carry this pain if Jesus already carried it for me?

He went ahead to say that there were times when he taught this scripture in Kenneth Hagin's healing school, and he would feel the Lord leading him and the participants to just confess 'Surely He hath borne our sicknesses and carried our pains...' and that after about thirty minutes of confessing this Word over and over, he would see the Holy Ghost descend on people and they would get healed.

Honestly, I'm not doing the summary of what Keith Moore preached any justice. I implore you to please trust God, go to the website, download and listen to this message; following the directions below. It's a five part series and the one I refer to is the first in the series. Even if you're not suffering any medical condition, still listen to it…you may have to recommend it to someone.

Go to ➔ www.moorelife.org/ ➔ free downloads ➔ series list ➔ By His Stripes

I bet you know what I did next. It was now time for me to act on what I'd just heard; it was time to trust God. I waited patiently for the message to come to an end and as soon as it did, I picked up my Bibles (electronic version and hard copy), went straight to my husband's study, and shut myself away from everyone and any possible distraction. I even switched my phone to airplane mode. I was determined in my heart that I would not step out of that study or talk to anyone until I was healed. Honestly, I was mentally determined to spend forty days and nights in that room till healing came. Somewhere in the crevices of my heart I knew it would not take that long because everyone who was healed by Jesus was healed within minutes, not to talk of now that I have the Holy Ghost as my assistant and Jesus as the High Priest over my confession.

You see for me, it was now or never. So I shut myself in and spent a few minutes worshipping and thanking God through my unbearable pain. Then I spent the next thirty minutes confessing 'Surely He hath borne my sicknesses and carried my ear pains. And with His stripes, I was healed.' Then I prayed in tongues for not less than thirty minutes. Then I thanked God for my healing and repeated the cycle all over again. As I confessed, prayed and praised I created a mental picture of the woman with the issue of blood whose mind was resolutely focused on touching the hem of Jesus' garment (Mark 5:25-34). Even though our stories are different, I feel that her fierce determination mirrored my own somewhat.

My people, midway into my second or third (I don't remember which) cycle of confessing, praying and giving thanks, I got healed! In other words, four to five days of absolute torture ended within four to five hours in God's presence and trusting Him alone to take this pain away. I can't even pinpoint the exact time the healing took place. I just noticed after a while that the throbbing pain and headache had gone. I continued my prayer/praise routine but decided to carefully touch my ear (which prior to now was painful to touch) to see if the pain was truly gone…and it was truly gone. I was so elated that I decided to spend another thirty to forty five minutes expressing my gratitude to God. From that night to date I've slept (ear) pain free!

Now I know some of you may be wondering if I went back to the doctor…I didn't. The only way I can explain this is to say that I was deeply convinced in my heart not to go back to him.

Another thing I'd like to point out is that as much as I believe in divine healing I also believe that modern medicine should not be shunned completely. After all the same God who heals people who can't be cured by doctors is the same God who created highly intelligent people who brought modern medicine to life. Charles Capps of blessed memory would say, taking your prescribed medication alongside confessing healing scriptures does not in any way diminish your faith or prevent the power of God from moving in your life. Also note that every healing recorded in the Bible was peculiar to the individual involved; every single one was different. If you're going through any kind of ailment and you feel moved to follow the steps I took please do so. However if within a certain period the condition is still the same, DO NOT FAINT OR LOSE HOPE. Go to God and pray for direction on what steps to take next. Another way of looking at it is to remember the warning found on most drug sachets/packs, which reads, 'If symptoms persist after three to five days, consult/contact your doctor.' In this case, The Almighty is the Great Physician.

May the grace of the Lord rest on you now and always. Amen.

About this writer

NKOYO ITEGBOJE is a seasoned HR Consultant with over 12 years of experience backed up by records of superior results in a variety of challenging and multicultural teams. Her hobbies include writing short stories inspired by biblical events and listening to music.

She's married to Solomon Itegboje, President & Founder of 3D Impact Media West Africa, a marketing and advertising company located in Lagos, Nigeria with offices across West Africa. They live in Lagos, Nigeria with their two children.

CHAPTER 3

The Balm of Gilead

My phone buzzed with a message notification that Thursday. The young lady, whose name translates to Grace, worked as a Dental Surgery Assistant, efficient, young and vivacious. I hadn't heard from her in a long while, so I decided to call. A rather faint voice answered; she sounded almost unrecognizable. She said she had been dealing with bouts of ill health for over four years, and was now in her village. The doctors blamed sickle cell anaemia, an incurable blood condition. The physical pain and weakness from the sickle cell crises had become so debilitating she had to stop working. When all else failed, her family had taken her back to her village, where she lay bed-ridden. She was covered in bedsores from impaired physical movement, and the family had given up all hope. They were left with treating one complication after the other, facing a bleak future.

I asked if there was a Bible close by or on her phone, so I could share some scripture with her. 'Ma'am, I can't read anymore, I'm beginning to lose my eyesight. I have to wait for my brother to come back home to read to me,' she said. She had also had to sell her valuables including her smartphone, to help with medical costs. Like the unnamed woman with the issue of blood in the Bible, (Matthew 9:20–22, Mark 5:25–34, Luke 8: 43– 48) she spent all she had on physicians and medical care and was not any better but rather grew worse.

Suddenly, the Holy Spirit took over the conversation. 'Grace,' I asked, 'do you believe in Jesus Christ?'

'Yes Ma'am, you know I believe in Him.'

'Who do you believe Jesus is to you, personally then?'

'I know He is my Lord and my Saviour,' she answered.

'He is your Saviour. Saviour means rescuer, deliverer, helper, healer and more,' I shouted into the phone. 'In the Name of Jesus, stand up and walk!'

'I can't,' she said, 'they even carry me to the bathroom, or strip wash me.'

'I don't care about that, in the Name of Jesus, get up, stand up; you can do it in the Name of Jesus!' Almost in a daze I could hear myself shrieking at her, 'This is the Name of Jesus we are talking about, it's no ordinary name, stand up, stand up now!' At that moment I heard her screaming, 'Ma, I'm standing up!'

'Walk go to your front door, shout the Name of Jesus, just don't sit down, Jesus has done it for you!'

I was still shouting and she was too, as she gave an account, 'I'm moving, I'm walking, I'm at the front door now, Jesus, Jesus…,' both of us excited and in tears of joy. A little while later her mother called me. 'We came back from the farm and met Grace moving about,' she said. 'It's the first time in years she's stood unaided. She had made her bed, she had swept the room, and I didn't know what to say. I'm overwhelmed.' She burst into tears as she spoke.

'Let's just say thank you Jesus,' I said, 'I'm overwhelmed as well.'

Her father, a retired soldier, found it hard to come to terms with this miracle.

'You mean someone prayed for you, in the Name of Jesus over the phone, over 800km away, and you just got up like that? Is that all? How can this be? Could you have been pretending all this while? To have four years of suffering just end like that?' He was baffled. I was amused.

The next day, she phoned several times with updates. Her mother was delighted and giving thanks to God. Grace walked through the village wearing high-heeled shoes for the first time in years. Laughing, she acknowledged the surprised looks and questioning stares of the villagers, 'Is this really you? No, it can't be, how did this happen?'

'Yes, it's really me. I'm not a ghost. Jesus healed me.'

To the glory of the Lord she walked boldly into church on Sunday, testifying of the goodness of God and how the Name of Jesus trumped every medical diagnosis. In the afternoon of that Sunday, droves of people from other churches and neighbouring villages went to the house to see and hear for themselves.

The Lord is the same yesterday, today and forever, and Grace's story is one of an empathetic Father whose loving kindness and tender mercies are available for those who call on His name.

Exhortation

King Hezekiah had learnt about access to God and relationship with God, through several challenges of life. After being enthroned, he set about studying the books of the law, and implementing what he saw. He got rid of the idols and restored the temple. Fourteen years into his reign, Sennacherib, King of Assyria threatened the nation and captured some cities of Judah (Isaiah 36-37, 2 Chronicles 32). Hezekiah sent for prophet Isaiah and asked him to intercede on their behalf. God responded, Sennacherib's army heard rumours about attacks in their own territory, so they left Judah to go deal with that. Nonetheless, Sennacherib demonstrated his intentions to capture Judah, and sent a letter to Hezekiah, threatening fire and brimstone. This time Hezekiah took the letter to the temple and presented it before God by himself, asking for His help and mercy. He prayed,

Of a truth LORD, the kings of Assyria have laid waste all the nation. Now therefore, O LORD our God, save us from his hand, that all the kingdoms of the earth may know that Thou art The LORD, even Thou only.
— Isaiah 37:18, 20 (KJV)

God answered, declaring that He would defend the city to save it, and in the morning, 185,000 Assyrian soldiers were found dead. The corpses were there for all to see. That of course put a stop to trouble from the Assyrian front.

However, when there was peace in the land, Hezekiah fell ill. He was in bad shape. He was told by Isaiah that God had said that he should put his affairs in order, because death was imminent. Hezekiah turned his face to the wall, prayed and then wept. God sent Isaiah back to tell him that He had heard Hezekiah's prayers and seen his tears too, and with a promise that in three days he would recover enough to go up to the temple to worship God. (Isaiah 38)

The details of Hezekiah's experience with illness, and God's answer, are recorded in Isaiah 38. He said, 'Please Lord, remember, how I have walked before you faithfully and wholeheartedly and have done what is good in your sight…I thought until the morning He will break all my bones, like a lion: You make an end of me day and night…My eyes grow weak looking upward. LORD I am oppressed, support me.'

Finally, he declares, 'The LORD will save me; we will play stringed instruments all the days of our lives at the house of the LORD.' His prayer was answered. God healed him, and the pain and turmoil became a memory.

Hezekiah hoped in God based on what he knew of God through the reading of the books of the law and from the remarkable experiences of answered prayers. His thoughts initially went into a downward spiral at the news that death was imminent, but he brought himself back from the brink, and declared his expectation of God's salvation. He trusted in God.

In Matthew 15:26 the Lord describes healing as the children's bread. "Children" connotes relationship. The

Lord gives us permission to own Him as our very own Abba - Father. Bread is a means of sustenance, so there's an underlying thought that children can expect good things from a good parent. As Jesus said in Matthew 7:11(KJV),

If ye then being evil, know how to give good gifts unto your children, how much more shall your Father which is in heaven give good things to them that ask him?

The Psalmist said in Psalm 130:5 (NLT), 'I am counting on the LORD; yes, I am counting on him. I have put my hope in his word.' Here is the nub of going through pain to victory, moving from illness to healing: hope. Trust in the infallible word of God.

What does this mean practically? We learn of Him, we memorise the word, hiding the word in our hearts, to keep us from giving up. We pray the word. We persevere, following in the footsteps of those who through faith and patience inherit the promises. Hebrews 12:3 urges us to consider Him (Jesus) so that we will not grow weary and lose heart. Why Jesus? 1 Peter 1:20 says Jesus was made manifest in these last times, specifically for us. In Hebrews 1:1-4, we see that Jesus is the icon, the express image of God. Anyone who believes on Him will not be ashamed (Romans 10:11). That's a wide sweeping promise, enough to direct our focus on who He is and what He has done for us. As we consider Jesus, through studying and meditating on the scriptures, we are changed into the same image from one level of glory to another, (2 Corinthians 3:18) we get a sense of who we are in God's family and what God thinks of us — dearly beloved, so loved that He transferred us from darkness into light and calls us sons of God. (Colossians 1:13, 1 John 3:1). His love is not fickle; it's an everlasting love (Jeremiah 31:3). It's the love of the One that cannot lie. No matter how long or how dreadful, whatever it is, He is willing and able to turn it around for good, for those who trust Him. Even a long distance prayer from a willing vessel, can be used by Him to make a difference. Let's trust God to keep His promises to us. He is Lord.

Helpful Scriptures

Genesis 18:14, Jeremiah 32:17, 2 Kings 19-20, Psalm 125, Hosea 6:3 Titus 1:2, Titus 3:6-7, 2 Corinthians 3:18, 1Timothy3: 16, Romans 4:21, Romans 15:4, 1 Corinthians 10:11, Isaiah 9:6 – 7, Ephesians 1:18-19, Ephesians 2:14, Matthew 19:26, 1 Peter 2:9

About This Writer

CHRISTINE ESSIEN'S background is Law; she holds an L.L.M in Law and Development from the University of Warwick, England. A development consultant, facilitator and skills trainer, she's a mother of two. Christine lives in Nigeria with her husband of nearly thirty years. She contributes articles to magazines, devotionals and Bible studies.

CHAPTER 4

Despite My Pain

I was introduced to deep pain in 1986. I was 15 days away from my eighteenth birthday. My mum, I was told, had eaten breakfast, laid down on the living room couch to take a nap and never woke up. I am not sure I can express the way I felt as the meaning of what I was being told dawned on me. My first thought was 'Who will take care of Sholly now?' Yes, my then five-year-old sister was my main concern. Long story short, the hat fell on my head and while it was painful, I relished my new role. I loved my sister with all my heart and I think focusing on her helped me deal with the pain somehow or should I say, block the pain. Anyway, life moved on. We — my sister, my brother and I — grew up and we were fine.

When my Papa, my Prof, died, I was four months away from clocking 46 and that day — January 26, 2014 — I discovered that deep pain had levels. You see, in the three decades since my mother died I had come to believe in God and trust in His love for me. Sitting on the floor beside her coffin during her wake-keeping service back then in Calabar, I had made a pact with Him. I promised that if He could just fix things such that my baby sister and brother would be OK, I'd give my life to Him, for real. I asked Him to guide my Papa right and help me make good choices too. In return, I gave Him my heart and asked Him to be my Lord and Helper. Through the years, even when I was unfaithful, He always kept His part of the deal.

So, I couldn't understand why He would let Prof die. This was a man He had delivered from countless car wrecks over the years. Why did He let this happen to me now? How could He be OK with us being orphans now? It hurt like hell. I cried my eyes and heart out for weeks, months even. I still cry. My Papa was my Champ. He believed in me and was always proud of me. He worried about my skin when I was a teen, making me try all manner of face cleansers. He bought me my first bottle of perfume, Anais Anais. Who would call me at a minute past midnight on my birthday now? Who would be my first New Year's Day call? More importantly, why had all my prayers for Prof to get better 'failed'? Why didn't God hear me? Why didn't God heal him and renew his strength?

'Just trust Me.'

I didn't have to ask who had spoken. I knew it was my PapaGod. I was on my knees in Prof's house in Ekiti on the day of the Service of Songs, February 28, 2014, crying and praying for help because the team that was meant to prepare the space for Prof to lie in state was nowhere to be found. I knew it was God speaking, but I thought He was asking me to trust Him over the lateness of the vendor that still had not arrived at almost past one in the afternoon! When would they get to Ikerre? When would they begin to set up? The service was to start in less than four hours! However, being God, He was not responding to my current physical reality. He knew what my real issues were. He was responding to my heart's cries.

'Prof is fine up here. Back to his youthful, sporty self. He can see and he can walk. Trust Me. You don't want him back.'

It was hard but over time I let it go and decided God knew what He was talking about. Still, two deep wounds were now seared into the skin of my heart. I was now an orphan. The family I had grown up knowing was now down by two. But at least I had my Sholly, my Tokunbo, my Aunty Silifa and my other siblings. For them, my husband and children, I decided to keep doing life.

Then life slapped the lights out of me again!

On December 28, 2016 at exactly 11.36am, I got a call. It was my sister, Sholly's husband, and he was telling me she had died. I am sure the walls of my office will never forget that day. My screams tore through the building.

The pain of losing my parents was nothing when compared to how I felt, and still feel, about Sholly's death. For weeks, I'm not sure I knew who I was or where I was. On the outside, I functioned and looked like a normal grief-struck woman but on the inside, I was worse. I was a spiritual wreck. All I could say in prayer was, 'Papa, help.'

You see, I blamed myself for Sholly's death. The last time I spoke to her, it was a Saturday and I was on my way to a wedding so our conversation was hurried. I promised to call her back. I didn't, but still chatted with her on Facebook on Monday. Her final response came in on Tuesday. Wednesday, she was dead. I'm her sister. I am her mum. We were so close. How could I have missed whatever it was that led to her death? How could I not have 'heard' her cry for help? Why didn't God help me hear? Why didn't He help Sholly? Why didn't He stop this? Didn't He know how much I loved her? All these years, I entrusted her to Him. He never failed then so how could He watch over me for 31 years and then sit by and let this happen? How could I ever trust Him again?

None of the above thinking was helped by all the craziness going on in Poland. Sholly's husband deciding to cremate her body five days after her death; then refusing to wait for me and my family to get there before doing so. How is God by my side and allowing this level of disrespect happen to my family? Sholly's husband would not let anybody see her body. We did not get details of the burial. We basically had no say in anything! The final straw was finding out that her ashes were buried! Come on! Who buries the ashes of a loved one? I was losing my mind along with my trust in God. And nobody knew it but me.

Salt gets her trust back (and her mind too)

Ah! I know the Holy Spirit of God is real. I say this because Sholly's death 'killed' me on the inside but God through His Spirit resurrected me. It was slow and is still an ongoing process but it did not begin till I learned to trust God again. Oh, don't get me wrong; I 'formed' like I still trusted Him. But I did not. I was mad at Him. Yet God, being so good and so kind, waited for my angry pain to abate.

I wish I could say I prayed a lot. I honestly did not. However I said 'Amen' many times, because there was plenty of praying going on around me.

I wish I could say I was seeking God in His Word a lot too. Nope. I was not. I was too busy advocating and trying to get justice for my baby. But I didn't miss church. And I played God's Word and inspirational music constantly and very loudly too. I did both mainly to frustrate the devil but you know, that was what God used to save me. He'd talk to me through the one random word I would hear or through the lyrics of a song. Every service I did attend, He'd send me a word.

And it's those little divine rays of hope that gradually began to work on my heart as we started planning for Sholly's Service of Songs scheduled to hold in February 2017. God has given me so many words to hold on to but the most important one has been, 'Just obey'. Yes, that's how I got my trust in God back. I just obeyed. Let me explain.

You see, there were many times I wanted to act in the flesh. To be honest, I did. I fought my MGM (Mighty Good Man, aka my husband) many times. I just felt all his 'calm down, let's be reasonable' statements suggested a total failure to understand my pain. He was being wise. I was just hurting so bad. I cursed out the whole Gaska family at least twice. I even had very foul thoughts about some members of my own family too and I spent many days crying my eyes out in utter hopelessness but in my quiet moments, I would always hear God calling out to me.

'Just obey.'

So, I obeyed.

Why?

It's simple; because God loves me.

One of the 'words' God sent me consistently was 'I love you. I love Sholly.' And then He would organise events in the physical to prove this to me. People showing up at my house with cooked meals; colleagues leaving work to come spend their lunch time with me; and my goodness, just looking at the sheer number of people that rallied round to support our 'Justice for Shola Gaska' cause. God used all these and more to convince me of His love and the moment I began to let my heart feel again, I was so grateful! All I wanted to do was thank Him and prove my love for Him too. And what is the best way to show our love for God? Yes, you obey Him.

> *If you love me, obey my commandments.*
> *— John 14:15 (NLT)*

And to obey God, one cannot obey the devil. So, I had to ignore the enemy and refuse to buy all the lies he was selling me: 'You will never find peace or really smile again so why bother? The truth will never be known. Even if people over there know the truth, they will not speak up; so why not just give up and give in to the darkness within? Fall in a heap of tears and give up. Roll over and stop fighting...'

And some days, the invitation did lure me; it just seemed so much easier. But no, I refused to give in.

I must emphasize again that I was not and still am not able to obey because it's easy or because I'm strong. No, I'm able because the Holy Spirit, as my Enabler, is real! The moment I leaned into God, He took me over and has been my Helper since then.

> *And the Holy Spirit helps us in our weakness. For example, we don't know what God wants us to pray for. But the Holy Spirit prays for us with groaning that cannot be expressed in words.*
> *— Romans 8:26 (NLT)*

He comes alongside me, and helps me 'bring my trust back' in simple obedience to God's Word. God's Word says to trust Him.

Trust in the LORD with all your heart; do not depend on your own understanding.
— Proverbs 3:5(NLT)

I chose to take this as a command; not a suggestion.

If God says to trust Him over Sholly's matter, then I must. If God assures me that justice will be done in His way and His timing, then trust I must. If God asks me to relax and believe that He knows the end of the matter from the beginning of it, then I don't need to know anybody at Aso Rock or fly to Poland to fight anybody. My God, the Ruler of the Universe, is fighting for me. And I know He will win and all of this will work out for good. That's His promise.

For I know the plans I have for you, says the Lord. They are plans for good and not for disaster, to give you a future and a hope.
— Jeremiah 29:11 (NLT)

And He isn't speaking only to me. He is saying the same thing to you now and it is my prayer that, right this very moment, our God of hope will fill you with all joy and peace as you trust in Him, so that you may overflow with hope by the power of the Holy Spirit (Romans 15:13).

In Jesus name!

Amen!

About This Writer

SALT ESSIEN-NELSON is a working wife, mum, and blogger turned published author. In 2009, her love for people and passion for writing gave birth to her blog ministry, The Salt Chronicles.

Salt is also the founder of the Shola Adefolalu Gaska Foundation aka the Sholly Smile Factory, a not-for-profit organisation determined to make the world a happier place, one smile at a time.

She draws her inspiration from all the life going on around her and believes, if only we would pay attention, there is a lesson to be learnt from all our experiences, good, bad and even the downright ugly.

CHAPTER 5

The Onion Hang-up

Settling into my space, a corner on the floor by the eastside of the altar in the mini chapel adjoining the auditorium, I responded to the invitation extended by the speaker to get alone with God; to hear Him share His heart in this place of rest. It was my first year in the seminary, at the Retreat Centre during the winter retreat. The speaker had been talking about the 'Sabbath Rest of God'.

I had barely snuggled up in my corner of choice when I heard these words, loud and clear, 'You have become an onion.'

'What! Did You just say that, Lord? What d'you mean?'

My mind raced with questions by the dozen. To my pessimistic mind, God was saying I stank. Only the strong smell of onion pervaded my mind. I could not imagine anything else. This was fast becoming a place of unrest!

God was surely drawing me into rest, but not like I imagined. He was stripping me of what was keeping me from resting, the citadel where I was locked up. He needed to strip off the mask that was hiding the real me from living the full life He had ordained for me.

That utterance boggled my mind.

'What exactly d'you mean Lord?' I asked again. 'Am I a stench to You?'

In my heart I sensed Him smile.

'By no means child.' He responded. 'It has nothing to do with your smell.'

Then He sent me on a research trip. He wanted me to find out the properties of an onion. That in itself was never anything I would have embarked upon.

'What qualities could an onion have besides it being a savoury ingredient?' I thought to myself. I brought out my phone and googled 'onion'. Boy was I astounded by what was staring back at me from Wikipedia! This pungent bulb does pack a punch!

Life-giving properties? Who knew! Apart from the nutrients, which as a vegetable it would naturally contain, I never reckoned it as anything special. Its culinary use, for which it was famous, was all I ever associated it with. I was oblivious of the healing properties of the little red, white or yellow vegetable. I discovered that even variants of the indomitable cancer stood no chance with this little trooper. Among athletes in the 1st century, it held center stage because of its 'fortifying' capabilities. Wow! An onion had all these properties? I had underrated it.

Captivated by what I was discovering about this little gem, it earned my respect. But what was the comparison, I wondered. He said I had become an onion. Then He caught my attention on its 'suit', a thin sheath, shredded often in places and barely able to cover this gem of a vegetable.

Then He began to speak to my heart. He told me that He created me just as He wanted me, tender, compassionate and easy-going. He knows my reservations about a lot of things, yet I never shy away from stepping up to do anything I believed He was asking of me. He knew how timid I could be, yet I adopted the motto, 'Do it afraid!' He knew how I was sold out to pleasing Him, but for this one thing: I wore a 'hard' exterior that tended to make me inaccessible to people.

Sigh! That hit below the belt!

He said, 'You are curtailing people from experiencing the life-giving qualities I deposited in you by hiding behind a brittle sheath that can't protect you, because you don't want to get hurt. Will you trust Me to protect you even when they hurt you?' He asked. 'Will you give Me a chance to be your defence?'

I broke down and wept.

He drew me into His embrace and allowed me to be rid of the pain in my heart. I had been hurt several times and I thought I had myself safely tucked away in this 'safe' fort where no one could get past my moat. My heart was cloaked (so I thought) in this secure place where vulnerability would have no access. And there it was, my brittle sheath as He just revealed, all torn up by love, His love.

I loved people, but also had my barricades up, barring them from getting past the surface. I didn't want to risk rejection. I did not want to contend with scraping up my shattered heart once someone broke and trampled on it.

A middle child, I was the family peacemaker. I learned to be neutral. I was not a popular gal in school either. I had trained myself to be content with my own company. Solitude was my hiding place.

Here I was, about to start my seminary training, preparing to step out to answer His call on my life, and He invited me to walk on water right away! He was requiring a new level of authenticity and complete vulnerability. This encounter lasted less than an hour, yet it felt like an eternity.

I knew what He was asking of me was the right thing to give up. I offered it up in prayer, and right away, the weight melted. I felt lighter. My heart and mind felt less laden.

I got up from this place of encounter and rest feeling refreshed. Yes, He had brought me into rest when I ceased the labour of holding up my brittle sheath.

I thought this was our private encounter. Little did I know He would ask me to go public right away. Psalm 105 says His Word will test us. I thought He would ease me gently into this new dispensation.

When we reconvened, the speaker asked for volunteers to share their encounters with the Lord. I clammed up. Not in a million years would I divulge that secret place experience! But no, He had a different idea.

He elbowed me forward. 'Share,' He said.

'What!' I whispered sharply.

I knew better than to keep up my argument; my typical response whenever He requested anything of me that would put me on center stage.

I raised my hand and shared my story.

I thought that was the end of that. Soon afterwards, during one of my 'Heart of Worship' classes, I was to bring the opening devotion. When I inquired of Him what He would have me speak about, He said — you guessed right — my onion hang-up story. It was not any easier, but this time, I stepped up quicker and I shared.

During our coffee break, at least three of my peers came to thank me for my vulnerability in sharing my story. They shared with me their own stories of identity struggle. They felt encouraged and bolstered to step up and step out. I was grateful that I obeyed. I saw what He said about what He wanted to use me for.

Then came another test of my trust and release to His grace, love and the protection of my heart. I was nominated for a position on the Students' Council. Shock was a tip of the iceberg compared to what I felt. The irony of it and the demonstration of God's sense of humour It was a position as the community coordinator.

Freaking out, I thought, 'Who knows me here? I don't talk to majority of the people here! I am even older than most people.' My mind churned out reasons why it couldn't be.

'I'm having none of that,' I took my stand. Alarm bells were going off within me! Apprehensive, I started erecting my wall of defence again. Surely, my reasonable response would be 'Thanks, but, no thanks.'

Quietly and firmly, He said, 'You'll allow your name to be put forward for the elections.'

'But what if no one votes for me?' I debated.

'Then, you'll not take away their right to reject you,' He said.

I had never heard anything like that before!

In obedience, I accepted the nomination and at the end of the day, I was elected! I was more in awe of God than in disbelief of the result. This was my personal parable. I saw what He was trying to teach me about pulling down my personal defences and allowing Him to be my shield.

So, I progressed in my odyssey into trust. Still work-in-progress, I continually grab His trust opportunities for me.

Love misunderstood

Understanding that His thoughts towards me are good and His plans for me are not to bring me harm, but to set me up for prosperity, (Jeremiah 29:11), I cannot but think of the rich young ruler in Matthew 19:16-22, Mark 10:17-22, and Luke 18:18-23. The fact that all three of the synoptic Gospels picked up on his story, held up a sign for me to pay attention to what Jesus was teaching this man.

The Bible records him as a man of influence and great wealth. There are so many like him today, whose trust is in their abilities and accomplishments, or something they hold dear. These have become their gods and they are reluctant to give them up to follow the one true God in trust.

To address his 'doing' mindset, and maybe to expose his reliance on his status, Jesus told him to sell all his possessions, give to the poor and follow Him. This was devastating to this young man, and goodness gracious, he missed the point, and he walked away!

Jesus was inviting him to inherit true Kingdom riches, but he would not take the risk on trust. He failed to understand the love of the Father and His prosperity plan for His children. He only heard loss; he failed to pick up on the gain that was being offered him.

The rich young ruler missed the point of the trust swap Jesus was asking him to make. His trust was in his own ability. God is not opposed to affluence. You only need to revisit the description of heaven to know He loves His bling!

He did not grasp the fullness of God's love for him. The love that seeks to give, not take. As much as this man had kept all the laws, Jesus pointed out to him what he lacked and was offering him the antidote, but he was consumed by the notion of loss. He ignored the advice of Solomon in Proverbs 11:28. He fell when he turned his back on that invitation.

His riches were his defence, his world.

Unknown to him, this was actually an invitation to become more (1 Timothy 6:17-19). Without a heart that trusts absolutely, God cannot give His best to us. What the young man was looking for, was in Who was inviting him into a relationship.

Riches are uncertain and cannot be trusted! God alone gives true riches.

Lavished with His grace

Ephesians 1:3-14 invites us into the reality of the image God has of us; the names He calls us. Let these titles germinate in your heart:

> BLESSED, CHOSEN, HOLY, BLAMELESS PREDESTINED, ADOPTED, REDEEMED FORGIVEN, HOPEFUL, INHERITOR BELIEVER, SEALED

When you apprehend your identity in Christ, the deceiver cannot place insecurities on you. You won't need any mask to hide behind.

Be thankful for, meditate on, and accept the full outcome of the sacrifice of Jesus and all that was accomplished by the blood of Jesus. What the blood of Jesus obtained is sufficient to demonstrate the perfect and everlasting love of the Father, which was 'lavished' on you. That should inspire the confident assurance that you are no accident. God planned for you and has a purpose for your life.

Knowing how special you are, that He chose you even before you existed, should boost your morale. The One who matters most singled you out for Himself, and that should be a thrill!

Write out those titles, meditate (think, speak and act) on them daily. Continue in them till they change the image of you that you see on the inside. REST in and be satisfied with His love for you.

About this writer

BOSEDE SANTOS longs to see Christians live fully in their identity in Christ. Bosede is an Associate Pastor holding a master's degree in Leadership and Ministry from the Ambrose University in Calgary, Canada.

Married to Ayokunle, both are joyful and honoured parents of two dynamic young men, Mayo and Ere. Bosede enjoys hospitality by welcoming people into her home. An avid walker and explorer of new pathways, she delights herself with exotic flavoured lattes and teas. A stirring minister of God's Word, Bosede is a writer and a practicing Life Coach.

CHAPTER 6

Jehovah Jireh

I had just graduated from the university and had obtained a prestigious internship with one of the most successful and popular corporations in the world. I was excited and full of youthful exuberance. I had to move out of state to work with this company for a year. This internship was great for job experience, but it did not pay too well. So, though I enjoyed the job and the great opportunity, I struggled financially. I was getting really frustrated and anxious, because bills were piling up. One day, I took all my bills and laid them on my table. I knelt down and prayed to God. 'Father, help me. These bills need to be paid and I don't know how I can pay them. You are the only one that can help me. So, I thank You for helping me, in Jesus' name. Amen.' I then got up and continued my day. I had left the problem with God and I felt a measure of relief even though the problem still existed physically.

That week, one of the supervisors I reported to began to talk to me about how hard things had been for him when he

started working with the company. I told him that I had
been struggling to keep up financially even though I loved
my job. He then asked me how much I needed; I told him
that it was a little over two hundred dollars. I was shocked
when he brought out his chequebook and proceeded to write
a check with the amount I had specified. I could not believe
it! He then said that I could pay him back once I was settled.
By now, my internship was almost over and I was moving
back to my state of residence. I told him that it would take a
while because I had not found a new job yet. He told me not
to worry about it. This was a good man that God raised to
help me. No strings attached. Some men would dare not
help like this unless sex was involved. This was The Hand
of God. I was so amazed and extremely thankful to God.
My brother also called me up to check on me and decided to
take care of two of my bills. Before I knew it, every bill I
had laid on the table for God's intervention, had been paid.
That's when I knew that God truly cared about me and I
needed to love and approach Him more. I needed to trust
God not only with things I felt that I could control, but
things I had no control over.

Christianity is all about faith; trusting that a God we cannot
see is real and that He means what He tells us in His Word.
God cares about everything that has to do with us. He is
aware when we struggle in lack and He is aware when
things are going very well for us. He wants to actively be a
part of our lives. Many times however, we behave like He is
not needed and we can figure things out on our own. This is

an exercise that I continue until this day. I lay out my finances before God, asking for His help. When my account is running low, I tell God all about it and thank Him in advance for depositing some money in it. God owns everything. Why should we spend time worrying needlessly about things that we cannot control? Why not hand our lives and everything that we have over to God?

When my son was a baby waking up for nighttime feedings, as soon as I picked him up he would stop crying, but his mouth would be moving in expectation. He knew exactly what was coming next — his food! As soon as he received his food, he would relax in the crook of my arm and eat to his satisfaction. The amazing thing is, he kept his eyes closed throughout. He knew that when he cried, I would pick him up and feed him. He did not need to open his eyes to see this, he just trusted his Mummy. This is how we should be with God (blind faith). We cry out to Him and trust that He will deliver us. As a loving parent, of course He will deliver us from lack or whatever we are struggling with.

In the U.S, when there is an emergency we dial 911. The 911 go-to scripture for worry in The Bible is Matthew 6:25-34. Anytime I read this passage in The Bible, I am comforted and rejuvenated. Jesus took the time to teach on worry because it is something that affects all of us deeply. Our Father in Heaven wants us to put our trust in Him. Not in the salaries that we make from our jobs, but in Him. It is very distressing to lose a job. You begin to worry about how to make ends meet. The truth is, it is not up to us to figure out how to make ends meet. It is up to God and it is described so beautifully in this Bible passage. So, whenever you are worried about what you lack in your life, visit this scripture and be encouraged. God is aware about all that concerns you and He will kindly provide all that you need according to His riches in glory. And God is very rich. His wealth cannot be measured. We are His children, so we should be cognizant of who we are. Our Heavenly Father will always provide for us. He gets us through each day with our daily bread. He is a faithful God.

Be anxious for nothing, but in everything by prayer and supplication, with thanksgiving, let your requests be made known to God; and the peace of God, which surpasses all understanding, will guard your hearts and minds through Christ Jesus.
— Philippians 4:6-7 (New King James Version, NKJV)

Whatever lack in your life has caused you to worry, give it to God today. His peace will saturate your very being, letting you know that He is working it out and will provide for you. Trust God with everything that you have. Build an intimate relationship with Him by studying His Word daily and praying to Him daily. Share your life with Him. Express your joys, your fears and your pains to God. He listens and He deals with all our troubles.

In my distress I called upon the LORD, and cried out to my God; He heard my voice from His temple, and my cry came before Him, even to His ears.
— Psalm 18:6 (NKJV)

Psalm 18 is a powerful chapter in The Bible that shows the love of God for us and how He goes to battle for us. It displays the intimate relationship King David had with God. We must seek God out and truly relate with Him. The God who was there for King David is the same God that is here for us today. He hears us when we pray and answers our prayers.

Always rebuke negative thoughts from the devil. Spend time also praising and worshipping God. It is such a relief to hand over our problems to a loving and caring Father. Just as children seek out comfort, love and advice from their parents, so should we be with God. He loves us so much and He will always make a way for us. To God be all the glory forever and ever. Amen.

About this writer

PASTOR BELLA ALEX-NOSAGIE is the President of Pastor Bella International Ministries (www.pastorbella.com). She is a minister of God in Word and Music. She is called specifically to prepare the singles for marriage and to educate the married on how to glorify God in their marriages. She is a part of God's clean-up crew to perfect His Church for His coming.

She is an author, speaker and singer who delights in God and is excited to serve Him. She is married with two children and resides both in the USA and Lagos, Nigeria.

CHAPTER 7

Even Through My Pain and Loss

T*he Lord is close to the broken-hearted and saves those who are crushed in spirit. — Psalm 34:18 (New International Version)*

The 8th of May, 2017 is one date that will remain indelible in my memory for years to come.

It began like any other Monday. I had finished dressing up and was getting ready to go to the office with my younger sister, when our Group Managing Director called my sister — my husband was away on a trip — and told her that my husband needed to speak with me, with him present. Apparently, my phone had been ringing but I did not see the calls until much later. When my sister relayed the information, I was somewhat bemused and I wondered what my husband would want to speak to me about that required the presence of a third party. I came out of my room to meet him in the sitting room, and then he dialled my husband's number and handed the phone over to me. My sister and I exchanged worried glances, and I remember my heart rate increasing.

'I'm sorry, I have bad news: Daddy has passed on.' Those were the words I heard from my husband, and while I waited in stunned silence for the import of what I had just heard to sink in, he added, 'I am coming straight home. I have cancelled my planned trip to Uyo.' He had been in Port Harcourt and the plan was that he would go to Uyo from Port Harcourt that Monday to see my dad, who had been in hospital for a little over a week. We had been told that he had greatly recovered. My younger brother who had travelled home to find out how he was faring, had been preparing to return to his Lagos base on Tuesday, not knowing that Dad would pass on that Monday. When my younger sister saw the horrified look on my face, she whispered, 'Is it papa?' I nodded speechlessly, trying to hold back the tears that were threatening to pour in torrents down my face. She asked again, as if to be sure, 'Is he dead?'

I nodded miserably, unable to speak. She stood up dazed, hesitated a bit as if she wanted to sit down, and then ran to her room. Our GMD and I rushed after her. She fell on the floor and began to wail like a baby. She struggled to push herself under the bed, but it was too low for her to fit in.

Momentarily forgetting my own tears and pain, I tried to hold her to no avail. She just screamed and screamed. I took my phone, thinking of whom to call as I shouted at my sister, 'Do you want to die too?! What do you want me to do?'

Then it occurred to me to call my pastor's wife. As if on cue, she picked up my call on the first ring and I quickly explained to her what had just happened — she could hear my sister wailing in the background. She spoke with me for some minutes, trying to get me to calm down, and then asked to speak to my younger sister. I went to her. She was sitting on the floor. I handed her the phone. Our pastor's wife spoke to her for several minutes and she gradually calmed down after the phone call.

I do not know how we got through those first few weeks of loss. I do not even want to go into all the drama that went into breaking the news to my mum, and later on our 96-year-old maternal grandma — our only surviving grandparent who had been praying throughout the brief period my dad was in hospital for God to take her instead and spare her son-in-law. On the morning that he passed, my mum had been preparing his breakfast to take to him in the hospital, not knowing that he had passed shortly after 5 a.m. However, she heard the news before my sister and I did, and while I was worried for her, she was also worried for us and had begged my husband not to relay the news to me on phone, because I had been very close to my dad. He insisted on telling me immediately, pointing out that it would be worse if I heard from someone else.

The next few weeks were a blur; I am sure that I was just going through the motions. I remember being angry at my dad at some point as I threw mental questions at him in my head. How could he die without saying goodbye to his 'Unyime Papa' as he fondly used to call me? How dare he not give me an inkling that he would not make it out of that hospital bed alive? The doctors had said the situation was manageable and that he would survive and I remember the last conversation we had — he kept assuring us all, that he would be fine and that we should not worry. According to my mum and brothers, who had been with him in hospital, he was getting better. They even sent us pictures to confirm their report. They also told me that he kept complaining about how his children were spending too much money on his hospital bills, but how much money could one spend to buy life? If there was life, there was hope of survival. The morning he passed, my younger brother had called him earlier. He answered the call and told him he was fine, and that he was at the reception. My brother had not understood what he meant. He called the carer who had been staying overnight at the hospital in order to attend to our dad, and asked if he had gone to sit at the hospital reception. She said he hadn't; he was lying on his bed. She later told us that he had said the same thing to her, that she should not disturb him because he was at a great reception. When the news of his death came, it dawned on my brother, and us all, what reception he had been alluding to.

I also had to battle with my feelings towards God. Ironically, the night before my dad passed, my younger sister, her friend, and I had decided to spend some time praying for my dad's health, and for the family, because there had been all kinds of near misses that week. My car brakes even failed, and one of my daughters kept crying over a bad dream she said she had about death. We spent close to two hours in prayer and praise-warfare and after the prayers I felt some relief. So you can imagine my horror when the news of my dad's death came the day after. I felt as if God had let me down. How could He allow my dad to die when I had entrusted his health to Him and had been so convinced that He would heal him? My dad had been a praying man; why would death snatch him away so soon and so unexpectedly? Who was death and what was his address? How come he was so powerful that he could not be tamed? I was emotionally wounded and felt a deep sense of loss.

It took a while to even begin to want to heal from the loss; I just wanted my dad back. One day in particular, I felt overwhelmed with my emotions and my husband offered to take me out on a drive around. As we drove around with no destination in mind — I just needed some air — my pastor's wife called me out of the blue and the words of comfort she spoke to me calmed me down to a great extent. It's been nearly 10 months since that fateful day, and there have been good days and bad days, but God has been faithful, even in those sore moments when I doubted Him.

What are my lessons from all the blows life has dealt me at different points? I lost my baby sister when I was in secondary school; she was just 4 years old. In 2009 my daughter was stillborn in the 8th month of pregnancy. And now I've lost my dad. I've come to realize strongly that the struggles of life are real, but so is God. He is a real and ever present help in the times of difficulties.

God is our refuge and strength, a very present help in trouble.

Therefore will not we fear, though the earth be removed, and though the mountains be carried into the midst of the sea;

Though the waters thereof roar and be troubled, though the mountains shake with the swelling thereof. Selah.

There is a river, the streams whereof shall make glad the city of God, the holy place of the tabernacles of the most High.

God is in the midst of her; she shall not be moved: God shall help her, and that right early.

— Psalm 46:1-5 (KJV)

It is indeed difficult to trust in a God who has made so many promises in His word, and still allows us to go through some harrowing experiences that shake that trust to its roots. I will not even pretend to have answers, but in my walk with God, I have grown in the understanding that, painfully challenging times do not negate the validity of His existence and love. I will never understand why God allows His loved ones to suffer such pain — it's beyond my grasp — but as the days go by, I understand better that we are just having a temporary experience on earth. Eternity beckons and Jesus is waiting to welcome us back home, but He desires for those who do not know Him to come to know Him personally, and so He tarries. Jesus experienced pain. He is not afraid of it but He walked through it on purpose and the scriptures make me understand that He is also touched by what touches me. He feels my pain and anguish and if I choose to let go and hand it all over to Him, He uses it to His glory.

Tragic things will happen as we navigate life, but God remains faithful. I had to turn to His word for succour and that was what kept me through those dark moments. I still do not understand why, but I can trust that He would not allow even a hair strand from my head to break off, without a reason. God definitely brings purpose to pain and loss (Romans 8:26-28). In the midst of the pain, I prayed to God. I vividly remember one of those days when I prayed through the pain. We were planning the burial at the time — that was another painful season — and we all got together in my mum's living room to praise and pray. The pain was real, but so was God's loving presence.

God desires for us to talk to Him and approach Him with our pains and struggles; He can handle them. Even when our circumstances change, the character of God remains the same. So I chose to pray and praise through the pain of loss.

Each time I remember my dad's final words, his very last phone call on earth to my youngest brother — 'Ekom, I am fine. I am at the reception' — it has helped me to keep an eternal perspective. My loss and pain pales in comparison to the thought of the grand reception that awaits each one of us, when our time on this earth is done. My dad had a foretaste (Philippians 3:7-14).

I read something profound somewhere once about the necessity of trusting the God you know, not the one you feel. You may not 'feel' Him when you are battling the pain of loss, but if you 'know' Him, you will be able to trust His intentions towards you and yours.

About this writer

AMB. UNYIME-IVY KING is a passionate God lover and an anointed scribe who sees her writing as an important calling and ministry, which enables her function as an influencer and change agent of society. She is a wife, mother, author, blogger, humanitarian worker and publisher. She is the Executive Director of the Save Our Women and Girls Foundation (SOW&G), a not-for-profit organization focused on creating social developmental awareness on issues that concern women and girls.

She is married to her best friend and husband of 15 years, Ubong King, and lives with him and their four children in Lagos.

CHAPTER 8

Giving Fear A Black-eye

Have you ever been afraid? I have been. Many times. I have been afraid of many things like the Bogeyman. In my childhood the Bogeyman was called Olokodana. I don't know why or what it was, but I was told it eats children and it lives at the back of my house, specifically behind my window. The fear of Olokodana was often used to lure us to bed early because it only comes out at night. So when darkness falls, fear would sit on my chest. It would remind me of something lurking in the dark. I would hyperventilate and go hide under the covers. I hated Olokodana with a passion, but I had no clue how to deal with Olokodana. Thus began the foundation of my many dimensional fears. I wrongly believed that the moment I become an adult I was free of the fear of the Bogeyman. No. I wasn't. Olokodana came back in the form of demonic apparitions that fully manifested even after I gave my life to Christ.

As a babe in Christ, I hadn't grasped the truth about my identity in Christ and the fact that I was seated in heavenly places far above principalities. I didn't know how to deploy the blood of Jesus or the name of Jesus. I didn't understand that God's angels watched over me. Many years ago in my bedroom (as I was about to pray) I saw what looked like an apparition in a red and black gown sitting on my windowsill. I bolted for the door. I mean, I was about to pray to God, yet that fear drove sense out of me. I barely slept that night. I was the night watchman. I wonder what God's angels must have been thinking at that point. Each night I would be paralysed by fear and unable to sleep without keeping one eye open. This went on for a few weeks. In church I would often hear 'fear not', but I was constantly afraid to sleep alone at night. I struggled with trusting that God's angels watched over me because frankly I couldn't see them, but I could see the apparitions. I wasn't sure whether that 'fear not' applied to my situation. Many people around me, including Christians, seemed to magnify the works of darkness more than God. They often talked about how one demon did this and that and those talks threatened my faith so badly.

I was getting fed up not being able to have a good night's rest. I wanted to be at peace, to sleep like everyone else. I was tormented daily with nightmares. It seemed there was no way out and my back was against the wall. It was like the devil challenging my faith and the God I serve. I needed to do something about it.

As I began to delve more into God's Word, at which point I was really studying the Bible for the first time in my life, I began to grasp certain truths. Every time I came across the phrase, 'fear not', I would get excited and jot the scripture down. I read in a book that 'do not fear' appears 365 times in the Bible. Now that's comforting. That shows that God knows that we will have occasion to be afraid. There will be many times fear will barrage our hearts and paralyze us. God doesn't want us to run from pillar to post, clueless and hopeless. He wants us to deal with fear. A lot of the things we're afraid of never come to pass.

Over time I read the Bible enough to understand that I didn't need to be afraid. Then one day whilst I was praying in my room, it seemed like something was present to make me afraid, to keep me from praying. I stood up and began pacing up and down my room. I wanted to reach out to God and at the same time deploy my memorised scriptures. I began to speak in tongues and pray in my understanding. I was afraid yet I wanted to win this battle. I didn't want to run away.

The first scripture that dropped in my spirit was James 4: 7. 'Submit to God, then resist the devil and he will flee from you.' How was I to submit to God in this situation? I was clueless. Then I remembered Psalm 22:3, which says God inhabits the praises of His people. I looked upward and began to worship God. I broke into both worship songs and words of adoration.

That was the very first time; I 'sensed' more of the presence of God than the demonic presence. That gave me boldness and I delved more into worship. I was having such a wildly fantastic time in God's presence. Then, the words, 'Now speak', dropped in my spirit. Speak what? I shrugged. I didn't know what to speak or to whom. I heard the words 'Now speak' again, and simultaneously 2 Timothy 1:7 dropped in my heart: For God hath not given us the spirit of fear, but of power and of love, and of a sound mind.

Then the lightbulb went off in my head. I began to speak 2 Tim 1:7 and then I rebuked the spirit of fear.

That was it. In a moment, the fear ceased. I continued speaking 2 Tim 1:7 to the air for a while longer.

You can trust God when you're afraid. You can tell Him you're afraid of this or that. He will refer you to His Word. You will find comfort and rest in His words. What you're afraid of, He can take care of.

I overcame the fear of the dark. I overcame the fear of apparitions. I learned to lean on God. I understood that I can place my fears and concerns in the hands of my Father and He can take care of not just my issues but also my tomorrow. Sometimes it is a doctor's report or something serious. Whatever the issue is, you can trust God to not only be in charge but to take care of you.

Dear friend, don't be afraid. Take God at His word; place your hand in His and rest in Him. You will conquer your fears, as you trust in Him. When you're afraid, look to the word of God. Remember that God is at the helm of your affairs. Whatever you're afraid of, God already knows about it. Give your fears to God. God didn't give them to you. You are a bold and courageous woman. You can handle that situation. You can deal with it. The wind beneath your sail is God Almighty Himself. How can you be afraid?

Here are some scriptures to help you deal with fear:

Isaiah 35:4. John 14:27. Joshua 1:9. Matthew 6:34. Psalm 23:4. Psalm 34:4. Psalm 27:1.

About this writer

SOLA MACAULAY is an inspirational speaker, poet, editor, author and an avid reader. She is passionate about helping people understand, love and embrace God in simple practical ways that authenticate the Christian walk. She explored this theme in her books: Petals of Grace and Whispers of the Morning; inspirational journals. She is the founder of 'Faith Dames', an online magazine for Christian women. She's a graduate of English Literature with

postgraduate studies in Human Resource
Management and Leadership Development. She lives
in Lagos with her husband and children.
(www.solamacaulay.com)

CHAPTER 9

I Was Better Off in Egypt

I left my 9-to-5 and high profile career to follow my heart.

The Lord was leading me into ministry; this was a new journey for me. I was literally walking on water.

Living outside the 9-to-5 meant there wasn't a pay cheque waiting for me at the end of the month. I had left the man-made financial system thinking that I was going to sink, but I had only fallen into God's system. God's system required trust.

I came to understand what it meant that the Lord who cared for the sparrow would care for me. In nature, the sparrow's provision did not come as a pay cheque at the end of the month, but it still came. It could come every day; it could come in high amounts today and not all tomorrow. It could come in the middle of the week, at the end of the month, or long after the end of the month.

Look at the birds of the air; they do not sow or reap or store away in barns, and yet your heavenly Father feeds them. Are you not much more valuable than they?

Matthew 6:26 (NIV)

I began to observe and understand God's system. God's system required faith.

I was living in a different realm. I would hear God speak to me in my sleep and when I was awake, and that was okay. But every now and then when I looked into my bank account I would wonder if I would make it for another month. God has been faithful. I've made it from month to month, and now year to year.

Now when any financial need comes up my automatic response is: 'The Lord will provide' or 'The Lord will help me.' And He always has.

One day I looked at my bank account and my money was running out. I panicked. I cried out to God, 'You told me to follow You! I was doing so well in my corporate job, now look at my finances.' As I was in this panic mode, complaining and grumbling to the Lord about what following Him had done to me, how it had been a disaster, and how I was better off in Egypt, He opened my eyes to see that I was not running out of money, but I was running into money.

What happened was I had invested in some stock. Because I was new to making money this way it didn't occur to me that all my cash had been converted into stock. So the Lord showed me that I did have money, but not in the form that I knew. My stock was my money and all I needed to do was to trade it and convert it back to cash if I wanted to.

If you're going through financial difficulty, understand that you have money. Look in you. Look at your skills, your education, your natural gifts and talents, and your supernatural gifts. Look at the things you have in your home, you have money sitting all around you. All these things are latent forms of money that can be converted into cash when you need to do so.

You need to become a master at converting what you have, your latent wealth, into cash.

Trust Him like a little child

The Lord reminded me about trusting Him just like a little child. In Matthew 18:3, Jesus said this to His followers who were struggling to believe Him: 'Truly I tell you, unless you change and become like little children, you will never enter the kingdom of heaven.'

Children are not complex people. Their thoughts are pure and innocent. They easily believe what they are told. They haven't experienced enough in their little lives to believe otherwise.

Their critical and analytical thinking process has not really been developed so they are not really able to use their mental faculties to reason God's voice out of the picture.

They are learning about the world around them, and are dependent on the significant adults in their lives to tell them the truth about life.

Trusting the Lord will be less difficult if we truly become like little children. The Lord tells us to trust in Him with all of our hearts and not to lean on our own understanding. He tells us to acknowledge Him in all of our ways, then He will direct our path. (Proverbs 3:5-6)

Our natural default, as God created us, is to trust. It is unnatural not to trust, so God wants to lead us back to trusting Him.

Adam and Eve lived in the dispensation of innocence, in Genesis 1 and 2 before the fall. They knew God was good. They trusted in His word by default and they lived in paradise. It was when trust was broken, when Satan injected thoughts of mistrust and unbelief into their hearts that they doubted God, fell into sin and were led astray, losing their God-given paradise and dominion. (Genesis 1-3).

When they stopped trusting God, they fell from glory. The way out of God's best was a lack of trust; the way back to living life at its best is to trust His character and His word. Trust is the same as having faith in God. God clearly states it's impossible to please Him without faith. (Hebrews 11:6)

He also tells us that the just shall live by faith, that is, trusting Him.

Where is your mind?

I watched a funny yet amazing video. It was an interview. The lady was on the streets of an African nation interviewing people.

She walked up to people, and her question to them was a very simple one, but their answer was profoundly funny. She asked them: 'Where is your mind?'

She wanted them to show her where their mind was, that is, what part of the body their mind was or where it was located. With confused looks on their faces and without any exception, each one of her interviewees pointed to their heart.

I thought hmmm, very interesting.

The English word 'mind' meant 'heart' in their native language, meaning their spirit.

Trust in the Lord doesn't really have to be difficult at all if we live by our spirits.

We were created to know things by our spirits, but the fall that happened, recorded in Genesis 3, brought about a change in God's divine order. It brought about a change in the order in which our spirit, soul and body relate with one another.

Our spirit knows God and trusts God, but our carnal mind is at enmity with Him, it's at war with Him, it fights against Him. (Romans 8:7)

With our spirits we contact God and the spiritual world, with our minds we contact the mental world and with our bodies the material world. God created our spirits to lead our minds and bodies, so that He could lead us into truth via His spirit that comes to live in our spirits at our regeneration, at our new birth.

Is it any wonder that Proverbs 3:5-7 calls on us to trust God with all of our heart (our spirits) and not to lean on our own understanding (our minds)?

Trust in the Lord with all your heart and lean not on your own understanding; in all your ways submit to Him, and He will make your paths straight.

- Proverbs 3:5-7 (NIV)

We are called to walk in the Spirit. If we walk in the flesh (with our reasoning faculties and our five senses not influenced by the Holy Spirit) it will always be difficult to trust God as the information supplied by both our spirit and minds often conflict, leading to us being double-minded. The Bible tells us that the double-minded person will not receive anything from God. (James 1:5)

As a Christian, we have the choice of either walking in the Spirit and trusting God, or walking in the flesh and not trusting Him. We must keep our eyes on God. Trusting God can come through familiarity with Him in prayer and in the word, but trusting God is also the work of the Holy Spirit.

Over-analysis can lead to paralysis

Personally, my challenge with trust has not had much to do with trusting God, it has to do with trusting me. Am I certain I have understood what He has promised? Do I understand the conditions of His promise? Are my self-interests leading me astray? Is the promise conditional or unconditional? Is its fulfillment dependent on God or is it partly dependent on me, and if it is, what am I supposed to do?

The capability of our rational and critical minds to overanalyse, often leads to frustration and causes spiritual paralysis. It's in times like these I remind myself that I need childlike faith, and that takes all the weight off me. I may not know all the answers to my questions, but I can hold His hand, knowing and trusting that The One I'm with knows all things, and I will not be let down or led astray.

I need to understand that there are things that I do not know, things I will never know, things too lofty for me to attain. I need to submit and trust God's leadership of me. I need to trust that He knows my way, and be happy living and following Him one day at a time, trusting that He will reveal all that I need to know when I need to know it.
I need to trust the fact that I am His sheep, I know Him and I know His voice. (John 10:1-5)

You need faith not money

As a single female minister, I lived in a 3 bedroom house, I planted and pastored a local church, and I actively reached out to my community. Many people in the community considered my home to be their home. My home was always full of people. It was an activity hub for The Gospel.

Little by little people moved into my house and it started to feel as if I needed a bigger house. Not only was my house the activity hub for the local people in the community, international ministers who were travelling from country to country and stopped in the UK, ended up using my house as a transit point.

I thought that I needed a bigger house after a little while. So I decided to ask the Lord for a 5 bedroom house, but since I wasn't actively in a job at that point in time I was thinking it probably would happen around 20 years down the line, when I would have saved up enough. I looked at housing prices, and what I had in my bank account was not going to do it.

Every morning when I woke up, I'd casually thank God for this five-bedroom house. I did this for about two years. Around the same time there was a young girl who lived with me and helped me with the ministry. She heard me making my confession every now and then, and she would eagerly say 'amen' to my prayers as she also saw the need.

Time passed, and I decided to move out of the house I was in and buy a house. To tell the truth, I wasn't really looking for 5 bedroom house. I wanted to leave because the streets had become so busy and the air was heavily polluted with fumes from cars. I kept on looking around the area where I lived but I could find nothing. So I started exploring further out to see if we would find something that was suitable. Eventually, an estate agent in a particular area called us and said they had a 5 bedroom house and wanted to know if I would like to see it.

I didn't even have the credentials to buy the house at that point. I looked at my bank account and my bank account was telling me it wasn't possible. I told the agents that I would look at the house, but it was sold before I could do so. I was so happy when I found out that the house was gone because I had cold feet. 'Thank God!' I thought.

Then a few days later the agent called me saying that another five-bedroom house was on the market. I thought, 'Oh God not again.' So I told the young lady who had been praying with me over the years about what was happening and what the estate agent said. She sensed my reluctance to go ahead and see the house. She said, 'You've been praying for this for several years. God is now giving it to you. Take it!'

Although I had asked God for this, I had not expanded my capability to receive it, so when what I had been praying for finally emerged, I panicked and struggled to take it. I didn't know the Lord was going to do it so soon. I was thinking 20 years down the line, when I had saved up enough to do it.

I was really thinking of what I had in my bank account, rather than what God had in his hand. The miracle was that everything went so smoothly that I bought the house in spite of my financial situation and moved in.

I then realised that it took faith, not money, to buy a five-bedroom house. Faith is the currency of God's Kingdom; money is the currency of the world's Kingdom. You will always have an abundance of faith, because God creates it and it's unlimited, but money is created and controlled by men. When you rely on money, you rely on your own ability and man's ability. When you rely on faith; you rely on God's ability.

Jesus told his disciples in Matthew 19:26, 'With man this is impossible, but with God all things are possible.'
Live the supernatural life. Become a dealer in faith, and then convert your faith into money. Other things that you need, as and when you need them, will be made available.

One eye on the Lord, the other eye on the storm.

Oftentimes doubt comes when we take our eyes off the Word of God and start looking at the world around us.

Peter knew Jesus, He knew Jesus' voice. He asked Jesus if he could come to Him, as Jesus walked on water. Jesus said 'Come'. It was a familiar voice, one he had slept with, eaten with, and spent time fellowshipping with, so he heeded it, and he walked on water.

But then there was another voice, the voice of his situation, the voice of the circumstances; this was a voice he had grown up with, a voice that he knew so well. He took his eyes off Jesus and placed them on his circumstances; the storm.

He stopped heeding the voice of the Shepherd, the voice of his Lord; he took his attention off the command of the Lord and gave attention to the voice of his circumstances that was now speaking to him so loudly. As soon as he did that, he began to sink. Jesus challenged him by saying: 'Why did you doubt?' (Matthew 14:31) When the Lord was his focus, he walked on water, but when the world became his focus, he began to sink. Doubt came with a shift in focus. The storm came to distract him. He who had walked on water began to sink.

Even as the word of God speaks to us, the world around us speaks to us as well. The newspaper speaks, our bank account speaks, our house speaks (something or the other may need to be fixed), our car speaks, our abilities and capabilities speak to us, and the future speaks as well.

All these things are usually not speaking the same thing that God is speaking to us; they may be speaking the total opposite.

Since I stepped out to follow the Lord, leaving my 9-to-5 job behind, I've had various things speak to me. They often tell me that I don't have enough money; that I have to spend money I don't have. My default response has always been that the Lord will help me, and He has always done so.

> *Do not fret because of those who are evil or be envious of those who do wrong; for like the grass they will soon wither, like green plants they will soon die away.*
> *— Psalm 37:1-2 (NIV)*

In the same way, all those other voices will soon die away.

It's imperative that the sheep knows the voice of the Shepherd and that it is the only voice they heed.

God is our authority. It's like being in the workplace with a boss telling you something and your work colleagues telling you another. The person to listen to is your boss. When you give the voice of God the authority that He deserves, recognising Him as the Almighty God, it matters not what any other voice is saying. His is the voice to listen to. His is the voice to trust.

About this writer

DAVIDA YEMI-AKANLE is an apostle sent both to the marketplace and to the nations. She is the founder of Friends of God World Outreach, and a visionary entrepreneur who is passionate about seeing Christians create wealth, and become financially free so that they can have more than enough to meet their own needs and fund the spread of the gospel. She is the founder of Kingdom Wealth Creation (KWC), the Kingdom Economic Empowerment Network (KEEN), and The Woman Entrepreneur Revolution (TWER).

Davida is a Bible teacher, as well as a prolific writer and author. She is also an advocate for vulnerable women and children; she is the founder of the Vulnerable Women and Children Action Group, and a co-founder of Say No to Domestic Violence and Abuse, (SayNo2DaV).

CHAPTER 10

His Miraculous Method

I was trusting God for healing. I had experienced and enjoyed 'miraculous' healings in the past. When I had a health challenge I went before the Lord and asked to be healed. He made a way for me during one of my church's healing service. I was overjoyed when I received my healing. My faith was buoyed at that moment and I knew then that I could believe God for anything.

Until a day came when I sat before the doctor and the diagnosis wasn't so good. I was ready for another faith adventure. After all, the same God who did it in the past is the same God who will do it again. I went before the Lord as in time past, and expected a 'boom!' kind of miracle through the laying on of hands, word of knowledge, or anything that would signify God's touch, but nothing happened.

Many healing services, miracle services, and prayer meetings later, questions began to form at the precipice of my mind. The big 'why' formed, and the response 'because' never followed. Not even a 'well, you see...' I was afraid to utter the questions, but in my mind, I had even charged God to court for not healing me the way I expected Him to. I spoke scriptures over my life, prayed, saw myself healed and nothing happened. My faith began to waver. It was a dance between trust and doubt. Did I do something wrong? Why couldn't God heal me like He did before? In fact, I added fasting to it even when I was too weak to fast, yet nothing changed.

I read many books on divine healing and rejoiced over testimonies of people who received divine healing. I read the Bible again and again; of Jesus going about 'doing good' and 'healing those oppressed by the devil'. Still, nothing changed. Months went by and the situation became critical. I panicked and for a while I wondered what I was going to do next. I wasn't sure if God wanted to heal me anymore. I searched inward for secret sins, unforgiveness and pointlessly religious prayers. I went through many other 'checks' and 'ticks' as though those were the qualifications for God's divine touch.

Despite the agonising pain and discomfort I had to live through, I decided to wait until my change came. Years rolled by and nothing changed my situation until one day things took a drastic turn for the worse. I needed urgent medical intervention. By this time, I wasn't sure if I was trusting God for the miraculous or trusting God for medical intervention or even trusting God at all. The diagnosis, which at the beginning wasn't so good, had now degenerated. There was only one way to go now. I could see clearly the options before me. I eventually submitted myself to the surgery I should have had years earlier, as my life now depended on it.

At this point, my prayer had changed from 'Heal me, oh Lord' to 'Heal me anyway You please. Just let me come out of the theatre alive.' It had to come to that. The hand holding on to God that had slackened over the years began to tighten again. I looked up to God. I needed to trust God again. My life depended on trusting God more than anything.

During my recovery period, as I lay on the hospital bed musing over everything, the Lord took me on a walk through scriptures. Jesus healed many sick and diseased folks. Some He spoke the word, some He spat on, for some He mixed spit and mud, and some even had to grab hold of His garment. Examples can be found in John 9:6, Mark 8:22-25, Matthew 8:5-13.

One thing was clear: no one size fits all. That I had to have surgery did not mean God wasn't at work or that He didn't plan to heal me. I needed to trust Him and His process. His method for this particular ailment was different. I failed to see that. I needed corrective surgery and He chose to do it the medical way. He chose to heal me with a mud. Otherwise, would He give the doctors the know-how to navigate the human system and fix things, then turn around and negate the same knowledge? There's a place for medical science and every once in a while God halts time and steps out of eternity into time just to change some things like heal, or allows us to step into the spiritual and receive divine assistance. The surgery was successful, recovery was fast and God perfected my healing.

I have learned that I ought to trust God in whatever method He chose to reach out to me. Trust is the key thing. I can navigate any route I choose to drive my daughter to school in the mornings, yet my daughter would sit in the car and not fret one bit. She knows that I will get her to school and on time. Going for a major surgery, coming out alive and healing from my surgical wounds is a miracle on its own. I learned to trust God in His own miraculous method, however He chooses. You should trust God in everything, no matter the peculiarity of His methodology. God is worthy to be trusted. You can place all your bets on Him.

About this writer

SOLA MACAULAY is an inspirational speaker, poet, editor, author and an avid reader. She is passionate about helping people understand, love and embrace God in simple practical ways that authenticate the Christian walk. She explored this theme in her books: Petals of Grace and Whispers of the Morning; inspirational journals. She is the founder of 'Faith Dames', an online magazine for Christian women. She's a graduate of English Literature with postgraduate studies in Human Resource Management and Leadership Development. She lives in Lagos with her husband and children. (www.solamacaulay.com)

Afterword

We hope you enjoyed reading this book. Did it bring back any memories or did it speak to your heart? Are you encouraged? Are you inspired enough to start thinking of your own trust journey with God? Did it further affirm and encourage you to trust in a loving, faithful and unchanging God. Kindly share your thoughts and stories with us. We would love to hear from you.

This book is the first in a part of a series called THE TRUST BOOK SERIES.

Would you like to share your own trust journey with us? If you would like to contribute to the next 'trust' book, kindly send an email to jedpubltd@gmail.com We will contact you with our submission guidelines.

We cannot wait to read your 'trust' story.

30612258R00065

Printed in Poland
by Amazon Fulfillment
Poland Sp. z o.o., Wrocław